AF280612

Self-love Journal:
Daily Questions to help you welcome more Positive Thinking, Motivation and Happiness into your Life

A Workbook to help you see what a Beautiful Human Being you are by helping you increase your Confidence, Gratitude and Self-esteem

BIBLIOGRAFISCHE INFORMATION DER DEUTSCHEN NATIONALBIBLIOTHEK: DIE
DEUTSCHE NATIONALBIBLIOTHEK VERZEICHNET DIESE PUBLIKATION IN DER
DEUTSCHEN NATIONALBIBLIOGRAFIE; DETAILLIERTE BIBLIOGRAFISCHE DATEN SIND
IM INTERNET ÜBER DNB.DNB.DE ABRUFBAR.

HERSTELLUNG UND VERLAG: BOD - BOOKS ON DEMAND, NORDERSTEDT

ISBN: 9783756807734

I am proud

Each page contains a sentence to finish
or a question to answer.
Try to fill out one page per day.
Be honest
and feel the love.

I am proud of myself for ....

I like myself for being...

What has become self-evident to me, although I should be proud of it?

What positive feedback did I receive in the past?

What is one of my favorite memories?

What is a reason my parents are or could be proud of me?

When did I work hard to get what I wanted?

In which moment in the past did I step out of my comfort-zone? Did anything change for me as a result?

I like about myself that...

What are the things my friends like about me?

What are the things I get positive feedback on when I meet new people?

I am ...

If I could, what would I say to my 5-year-old-self?

If I could, what would I say to my 5-year-old-self?

What am I grateful for?

What am I grateful for?

What part of my body do I like?

What did I love doing as a child?

Today you can simply write:
I love myself

Date:

I am strong because...

I like about my character that....

What could I do for myself next week?

When did I feel proud of myself?

Remember how that felt.
Feel it.

What advice would I give my friends, if they would be in my situation?

When I think about the last month, what could I be proud of?

What do I care about?

In which moment did I feel loved?

Remember how that felt
and take this feeling with you
throughout this day.

What do I like about the way I handle things?

When have I said something truly kind to myself lately?

Why should I be loved?

What am I getting better and better at?

What should I appreciate more about myself?

When I think about what has changed and challenged me in the last year, what can I be proud of?

What am I good at?

What person(s) am I grateful for today?

Date:

What might impress others about me?

What is my most recent 'step in the right direction'?

What can I love myself for?

What do I wish for?
Imagine with all your available power that it will come true.

By whom am I loved?

I like about myself that ...

When did I overcome my fear in the past?

When I think about how many challenges I have overcome in the last 10 years, what can I deeply and sincerely be proud of?

When I think of my daily life, what might be underappreciated?

What could I thank my body for?

What is something I like about me?

What is one of my favorite things to do in life?

Date:

What was I proud of 10 years ago?

Why could my friends think of me as a good friend?

I am strong because ...

What is my favorite memory of the last year?

I am grateful for ...

Imagine your younger self.
What do I love my younger self for?

I am proud of myself for...

Space for thoughts